The Great Property Ponzi Scam
Unlock The Truth, Educate Yourself, and Protect Your Investments

Richard Houston

Disclaimer

The information in this book is based upon my own personal opinion and experience. You should not assume any information or example in this book is necessarily relevant or applicable to your particular situation. This book is not meant to provide legal or financial advice and should not be relied on to do so. The opinions stated in this book are my personal views and are not intended as text on the legal or financial aspects of property investing, share investing or business in general, and should not be relied on as such.

While every care has been taken in the preparation of this book, the publisher will not accept any responsibility or liability for any error in the information contained in it, however caused. Readers are urged to seek appropriate independent advice from suitably qualified professionals for their individual needs.

All figures and statistics in the book are accurate at the time of publishing; however, they may be subject to change.

This book is fiction, except for the parts that are true or may come true.

ISBN: 1-4664-9611-8
ISBN-13: 9781466496118

DEDICATION

Even though I wrote this book, I certainly did not do it on my own. In fact, the information in this book comes from a range of people whom I love very dearly and who allowed me to do this.

To my loving children Beck, Destiny and Stefan, I thank you and love you all so very much. Thanks for all your interruptions and attempts to capture my attention.

To my darling Dragana, I thank you and love you for so much, but in this case for the numerous coffees and chats we have to analyse the world's problems and provide solutions. Your great insights and instincts really do help me to complete my understanding of this world.

(To the reader: if you ever get a chance to have a chat with my partner Dragana, you will understand everything I have said and know how understated I have been in my praise of her here.)

Thanks to all my loving family.

TABLE OF CONTENTS

ABOUT RICHARD HOUSTON

My name is Richard Houston. I am just an average guy who has taken the time to listen, look and learn. I have made more mistakes than anyone I know in life, and yet still, amazingly, I am here today to share with you my opinions and insights.

So what are my qualifications? Basically, I completed my High School Certificate in 1979 and attempted to obtain a Commerce Degree at the prestigious Melbourne University in 1980.

I learned early in my first economics class that I was not into this stuff and that there must be something more enjoyable to do with my time.

So I quit university and started my own business. I saw an advertisement in the "business for sale" column of the daily paper for a vending machine business. I went to see a man who said he had six vending machines located in local football clubs, and that they were making good money.

It sounded pretty good to a young man who wanted to make money, so I said I was in. He arranged a loan for $25,000, and thus I started my first business. To this day I still don't know how a young unemployed university student could get a loan for $25,000 from a major bank.

Well, the money came flowing in and within 12 months I had paid back the loan...and then *smack,* my first lesson in business. The government changed its rules and outlawed poker machines, and the business became worthless overnight.

Not to be deterred, I went off and got a job. I know, how pathetic of me, but hey, I was *just above broke* (JOB) and needed the money. So I did the right thing. I worked hard and saved money. I raised enough cash to buy my new business, a cigarette vending machine run.

I was confident that this time the government could not stop me. So off I went and bought the first five machines. In less than a year, I had some 20 machines stationed in local sporting clubs around my city.

Then it happened. The government stepped in again. It did not close me down, but they raised the prices to a point where the price of a pack of cigarettes was over $2.00 and my old machines could not handle so many coins. I had the choice of closing down again or spend thousands for the new machines that could handle the coins and notes.

The lesson I learned here was that technology can close you down as quickly as the government can.

By now, my decision to quit university was not looking so good. But still not to be deterred, off I went and began a career in finance. I started work for AVCO Finance (later bought out by GE Finance) and worked hard for two years until I became an assistant manager.

Along with the income from AVCO, my work at a second job at the cinema, and the money I received from playing football, I saved enough money to buy my first property and started living in it.

Now came my big move into banking. In 1987, just before the stock market crash, I started work with a major trading bank in Australia. I was fairly successful in my banking career, but I knew there was more.

Finally, in 1995, I left the bank with money in hand from my hard-earned savings and invested in a building technology, which my partner and I took to Asia.

Let's just say that the next four years was a nightmare. I went from owning a modest home and having a good income to nearly bankrupt.

We had spent all our money on getting a contract signed and sealed for 10,000 homes to be built in the Maldives, using our building technology, only to have the contract annulled by a certain Malaysian politician (who I think actually stole the deal).

Don't get me wrong—I am not blaming anyone for my mistakes. I take full responsibility for anything I do in life. But I did learn that doing business overseas is very dangerous, and there are lots of sharks out there who will eat you up and spit you out.

So it was with my tail between my legs that I went back to live with mum and dad. It was so embarrassing living at home with them when the debt collectors came knocking. To this day I feel sorry for my parents.

While I was overseas I did have one piece of good luck. Citibank rang me to say they would pay me $400 if I referred a person who subsequently obtained a loan from them. This gave me an idea. I did my research and saw that banks would soon start selling loans via third party salespeople like mortgage brokers.

I had no money and still owed my creditors over $100,000. Hardly the right start for any business, but I had a great idea and wanted to get it done. I was lucky enough to find a local investor who provided $50,000 in capital to build the software that would revolutionise the mortgage brokerage industry.

Over the next five years I went from nothing to generating over $1 million in profit and a business worth over $5 million.

My debts were paid off in full and my business was on fire. Then came the insight part. Someone I don't even know to this day sent me a video in the mail. Based upon the video, I started investigating what was happening in the financial world, and by 2005 I knew I had to sell my business. I did, and then three years later the 2008 Global Financial Crisis hit. My business was already sold. Good luck or good planning? I will leave that to you to decide.

The lesson here is that I have immersed myself in information and refuse to take advice from the mainstream media or the so-called experts. If I could see the GFC coming, why did experts not see it also?

That is why I am writing this book. The property market is just part of a giant worldwide Ponzi scam that will eat up and spit out anyone who does not wake up and start getting a real education.

And it was with this concept that my wife and I started Money Wars TV in 2010 to help people just like you get a real financial education, so that you can survive the coming financial Armageddon.

Take a moment and check out www.moneywarstv.com and the must-see documentary *Money Wars.*

Enough about me. Please sit down, get comfortable and enjoy reading this challenging and provocative book.

If you have any questions or comments, feel free to email me at richard@fintrack.com.au.

Chapter 1
TWO TRIBES GO TO WAR

The Worst Depression Since the Great Depression

Okay. Right off the bat, I am going to get you mad at me. I am going to tell you the truth whether you like it or not. You see, if someone does not start telling you the truth, then you will end up flat broke and in a food line.

Where are we today? We are in the worst depression since the Great Depression.

We have negative interest rates—yes, some people have to pay the banks interest to hold on to their money. Pretty alarming, isn't it? We also have real inflation of five percent to 10 percent. If inflation increases by two percent or more, we'll *really* have problems.

The depression is already here, with over 26 million Americans unemployed, riots in Greece, and sovereign debt problems worldwide. The world is in a real mess. It's time to start switching off the mainstream media and start looking for the truth.

Just to annoy you further, I'll say that this is a deliberate destruction of your financial future that is being played out right now, and one of your biggest assets (or liabilities)—your home—is on the line.

What we see today is like a 1923-style collapse on global scale, and the Obama administration is acting like the clueless German government did at the time.

Like it or not, an invisible conspiracy is being played out, and you have to be awakened from your zombie sleep.

Here's what I think is happening today. I challenge you to do your homework and prove me wrong.

The Banksters on Wall Street have created a property Ponzi scam that is about to destroy your wealth. The money in your retirement fund is going to lose value every year, as is the value of your home. I will explain and demonstrate this throughout the rest of the book.

Government statistics are being manipulated so as to keep you in the dark, and the mainstream media are right in on the scam. It makes me angry that this Ponzi scam is being allowed to flourish by the very people you have trusted to look after you.

A big lesson in this is that we all need to start trusting the government less and start taking personal responsibility for our own needs. Once you start looking after yourself, then you can start looking after others like your family and friends.

But if you continue to trust the Banksters and politicians, then you end up with nothing—and you lose your home!

So what will this mean for young people?
The more that governments around the world print money, the less that paper money is actually worth. That means a weaker econo-

my. So if you are a young person just starting off your career, you are likely to wake up one day in a new world, in an economy with very few jobs, and more young people than ever from all over the world vying for those jobs. You will work harder and earn less.

There is an upside for those who can raise money for property, as up until now you probably could not get into a property because the prices have been too high. In the future, houses will be much cheaper as this Ponzi scam plays out.

What will this mean for the family person?

Households for years have been using their homes like ATMs and going on debt-fuelled binge spending sprees. The whole premise has been that homes would always go up in value. As we have seen in Europe and America, this is not always the case.

So your home will be worth less. Later on, I'll demonstrate just how much less.

Your ability to transfer to another job will also be much harder as opportunities decrease. And your so-called retirement plans may well go up in smoke.

If you have not seen it as yet, please get the film *The Company Men* to see just how hard life could get.

What will this mean for the retired person?

You will not hear this from your financial advisor, but we are entering into a prolonged depression that will require you to have more of your own money to lean on for survival. Self-reliance is key.

If you leave your money in the share market under some managed fund or retirement plan, you will see it erode over time until it is virtually worthless. Your money on term deposit will be earning less than 3 percent if we have a deflationary depression. Or, good news: it will earn 15 percent if we have hyperinflation, although the actual money will be worthless.

So what can you do to protect your hard-earned money in your retirement? Well, a good start is reading this book and challenging the education you've had up until today.

The Perfect Storm is Coming

We are heading into a perfect financial storm that will either wipe you out or make you very rich—if you understand what is happening and what will happen in the coming decade.

This next decade will be the most challenging in man's history to date. Most economies can be described as being:

BOOM—Yippee, everything we do is magic
BUST—All is going to hell
STAGNATING—No growth

In every economy there is a price for a home, car or food. This is generally determined by terms such as:

INFLATION—Prices go up by, say, 10 percent per year
HYPERINFLATION—Prices go up by 30 percent or more
STAGFLATION—Nothing is going up or down
DEFLATION—Prices are going down by 10 percent per year

Now take a moment to ask yourself what *your* economy is doing, and how the prices of assets and consumables are doing.

My personal opinion is that we are entering a perfect storm or financial Armageddon, with *deflation* for assets like property, shares and cars, and *inflation* for consumables like food and energy.

The economy is going to go BUST as people lose jobs, asset values go down, and no one has a dollar to buy anything. The worse thing about this doom and gloom is that it will not be a "big bang" bust but rather a slow, cancerous 10 percent decrease year after year for the next decade.

So how does this affect property? Well, here I go on my way to challenging everything you have been told about what has happened, why it happened and what is going to happen.

In the next 10 years, over U.S. $50 trillion of assets will change hands, and for every loser there will be a winner. Which one will you be? By reading this book you may actually have a chance to decide which one you will become.

As a sidenote: many think that we should change the system and vote new people into our governments. Those are nice ideas, but will not solve the issues. I believe it is easier to change myself than change others (and I should know, as I have tried to change plenty of people in the past and failed).

Enough of that. Let's get into the nitty-gritty of this book so that you can either call me a crackpot or a guru by the end.

By the way, to give me a fair chance in this, please read the book to the last page, and even read it again if need be. It could save your family in the future. You might think I am a crazy person, but give me some of your time before you make that judgment.

Causes of Depressions

There are two main causes of depressions. One is caused by *deflation* and the other is caused by *hyperinflation*. Let's take a look at two depressions from the last 50 years.

The U.S. depression of 1929 happened when the U.S. was still on the gold standard, so the country could not print money. This meant that people who had saved their money were winners as the economy slowed and assets deflated.

The German Weimar Republic 1929 depression was caused by hyperinflation. Germany at this time was *not* on the gold standard; they had a *fiat* currency. (Fiat currency is paper money decreed by law as legal tender, not backed by any gold or silver, but rather backed only the guarantee of the government that printed it.)

So with no backing for their money (like gold) they just kept on printing money, and in the end they made their money worthless. In this case, anyone who had saved money became a loser.

There is an old story about the depression in Germany. Apparently a woman took a wheelbarrow of money to a bakery to buy a loaf of bread. She took some money and went inside to buy the loaf of bread and left the remaining money in the wheelbarrow outside.

When she returned outside, she found her wheelbarrow had been stolen, but the thieves had left the Reich marks (German dollars) behind. This comical story is an example of how hyperinflation makes your money virtually worthless.

A Decade of Crisis

The 2008 Global Financial Crisis has taken two years to reach most people, but by today nearly everyone knows there was a global financial crisis.

What people don't know is how to deal with this type of crisis. They pray to their politicians or God, and just hold their breath hoping that all will get better.

If only I had a dollar for every time someone told me that it will all get better soon! The minority have started to wake up and start getting educated, so that they can make changes to survive the next crisis.

The problem is that the next 10 years may be one of the most tumultuous decades in the world's history.

But most of the "sheeple" will cling to the past with notions of job security, saving money for retirement, and investing in property.

On a happier note, the next decade will provide massive opportunity to those who really do pay attention to what is going on.

I see more poor people!

As I meet more and more people, I just keep on hearing the same stories. People are struggling to make ends meet or get ahead in life. If you feel the same way, you are not alone. You are in the majority.

Many of these people were just average, what we know as "middle class," owning a home and a car and having a job.

Today as these people lose their jobs and their houses, I see more poor people. I also meet those who have adapted, and they are getting richer. The divide is getting bigger as the middle class is wiped out.

Thinking of property investment?

You have probably bought this book because you are thinking of buying a property, or just looking at what you might do with your home that is drowning in debt.

This is a great place to start the real debate about property as an investment.

This book is one of the few places you will find honest opinion and discussion that is not smothered in the rubbish that has been peddled to you for years by the media, property promoters, banks and politicians.

Property markets seem to be either going down like in the U.S. or becoming flat like in Australia. Investors are now worried not just about lower investment yields or returns from property, but also the notion that maybe property does not go up all the time as the property promoters claim it does.

Many property owners look at property values daily, the way some watch the share market. But what is the view of property in the long term? What will your property be worth in, say, 10 years?

Most people I talk to have a firm belief that property only goes up and up. Until 2008, they may have been right.

But if you dig deeper and unveil the curtain behind what has been really happening since the 1970s, you will begin to question whether property prices will go up forever!

By far, most people's wealth is wrapped up in housing, whether in their private homes or investment property. Therefore, what affects this market affects a lot of people.

Debt levels are high as people try to keep up with the "Joneses" and outbid each other for property. This forces up the price of a home. The person whose bank is more willing to extend the bigger loan gets the home.

There are two main groups with different opinions on the property market.

On one side is the majority: people who have bought into the BS by property promoters and believe that property is a great investment and that property prices are supported by population growth, low interest rates and a so-called chronic housing supply shortage.

On the other side is the minority of people who are starting to be skeptical about the true drivers of housing. They think that property worldwide is in a bubble fuelled by easy credit, artificial low interest rates, and first-time home-buyer incentives.

Once the main drivers of property are exhausted, as they are now, then this bubble will burst and the mass of people who were sucked into this Ponzi scheme will be crushed. Then the elite will come in and buy up their properties for a dime.

The Stakeholders

So who are the stakeholders in the first group that seem to want you to believe that property never goes down?

Start with unscrupulous salespeople like property promoters who sell you the property, and the mortgage broker who receives commission for selling you the debt on behalf of the Banksters.

I should know, as I was once a mortgage broker who made money by selling debt to people. I also at one time worked for a major bank.

Next come the banks, property developers, real estate agents… and don't forget the politicians, who know that if you feel wealthy because your house value goes up, then they may get your vote today.

The House of Cards

In many countries, a property bubble has replaced the stock market bubble. Sooner or later it will burst.

Most people believe that buying property is by far the safest investment you can make. This type of advice is offered by real estate agents around the world.

From Washington to Sydney, the topic of dinner parties has been increasing property prices and how rich we all may be. But one thing that amazes me is how little real research comes into play when looking at property.

In the past, most people discussed property as purely as a place to live in, rather than as an investment.

Since the 1970s, housing prices have skyrocketed, especially in places like Australia, Britain, Ireland, Spain and Sweden. Now the thin ice is crumbling, and below the ice is just cold water, which is where property will soon be.

How long can the party last?

U.S. Housing Boom and Bust

Scary headlines and scarier statistics have enveloped the American housing boom and bust that arguably may have been a catalyst for the Global Financial Crisis starting in the first place. I will just touch on some issues here, but there are warnings for all of us from this debacle.

In the U.S., the typical American is suffering. He had equity of 61 percent in his house back in 2001. Now, he's got a paltry 38 percent. And he's lucky to have that. There are 15 million homeowners who have less than zero equity. They're "under water" and still sinking.

Who are the players in this debacle?

Fannie Mae and Freddie Mac

The Federal National Mortgage Association (Fannie Mae) and the Federal Home Loan Mortgage Corporation (Freddie Mac) are the two government-created but privately-owned profit-making enterprises that bought and sold many mortgages that local banks sold to consumers. These two took up the gauntlet of "home ownership" through "affordable housing for all," especially for low-income people.

How ironic that the very people the government is trying to help—low-income or poor people, many black or Hispanic—are the very ones being most badly burned by the government in America, regardless of which political party is in the White House.

The Government and U.S. Regulations

The U.S. Department of Housing and Urban Development (HUD) was supposed to oversee and regulate Fanny Mae and Freddie Mac and thereby directly influence mortgage lending practices.

Add to this environment the politics of housing, whereby everyone desired a home of his or her own, regardless of whether the loan could be paid back or not.

A fundamental issue for the U.S. housing market was trying to provide housing for all, especially the minority groups who also had the lowest-paid jobs if they were employed at all. It became a national issue for all to have a home at an affordable price. But greed kicked in and destroyed those hopes.

The U.S. government sat by and let the monster it had created become even stronger, thanks to the Federal Reserve and other players in this mess.

The government was warned on many occasions that things were getting out of hand and that this property boom could not last forever. When it all came down with a thud, the political blame started.

It is nice for the social agenda and for people to feel better by providing housing for all, but the bottom line is that if you artificially stimulate housing growth via false demand and free easy credit to people who are in no position to repay loans, then you have just created a recipe for disaster in the future.

Banks

Next in this cast of characters were banks, who just could not help themselves. They had to lend out as much easy cheap money as they could, so as to improve their profits and keep the American dream going.

And with the use of lending insurance to protect them, the banks went on a crusade of lending without any fear of loss, and the prospects of making huge amounts of money. Remember Gordon Gecko's famous words in the 1987 movie *Wall Street?* Gordon's famous words were "Greed is good."

Mortgage Brokers

Next were the mortgage brokers, the salespeople who sold the dream to everyone. Remember that the demand was artificially increased by easy credit sold by eager salespeople (mortgage brokers) who, paid on commission, made more money by getting you into more debt.

These guys made false declarations of income, if they even verified income at all, and made the most of every application they could so as to be paid in gold by their masters—the banks. Banks then made massive profits on the deals, knowing full well that they might have issues down the track.

I remember taking courses on low-documentation loans, where the instructors advised that the clients could just declare what they earned rather than prove their income.

Another bank I came to know admitted that they did not verify the income of a client, as that was the mortgage broker's job. When I asked a mortgage broker about this, he said that income verification was the bank's problem. Not too hard to see some problems here…

U.S. Federal Reserve
The U.S. Federal Reserve, which regulated the system that allowed cheap easy credit and low interest rates, encouraged borrowers to borrow large sums of debt on overinflated housing that was supposed to rise in value forever. I will go into more detail later on this subject later.

Wall Street
Wall Street then took over the sales process by repackaging and splitting a basic home loan into so many parts that no one knew who owned what.

The rating companies like Moody's then came to the party and rated debts as "AAA" (the best rating a debt can have for safety) despite not really knowing what the debt was made up of. Many portfolios containing a variety of debt types in actuality were "spliced" with just enough AAA debt to be passed off as highly rated, when in fact they were made up of a variety of debts.

Once upon a time, a person wanting a loan used to roll up to a bank manager and beg him for a loan, after demonstrating the capacity to pay the loan back. This person generally had a 20 percent deposit, giving the bank collateral or security for the loan, and usually proved good standing in the community by being gainfully employed and having homed in the same place for years. Such a person was happy when the lender fixed the loan at 30 years.

Things have changed, with zero-down mortgages, honeymoon rates that revert to variable rates, interest-only loans, and low-documentation or even no-documentation loans.

Mankind has come a long way in the last 10 to 20 years, from a beggar of finance to a junkie for debt.

Adjustable rate mortgages started the problem in the U.S., on the backs of unscrupulous mortgage brokers using predatory lending practices, and banks who were keen to look the other way.

It is ironic that the U.S. Federal Reserve, which keeps statistics on all this, did not have a definition of the term "predatory lending practices."

But then again, maybe it is harder to describe what others do badly when you yourself have done far worse.

The Borrowers Themselves

Last but not least in this cast of characters we have the poor borrowers themselves. The victims of the government, banks and mortgage brokers, you say?

Not exactly. These fools knew that they could not pay back the loans. They were living in a world of denial.

If a person is self-employed and declares no taxable income, yet supposedly makes $100,000 per year paper, why would they need to borrow in order to buy property? Why would they not just use that real cash to do it?

They figured that one day the house would be worth heaps, and then they could just refinance again and continue the denial.

Worse still are the guys with no jobs who thought it would be great to get into a new home even though they had no way of paying back the loan. Later, many screamed that the mortgage broker had lied on the application (where the client had himself signed)!

జంసా

Chapter 2
WORLDWIDE BUBBLE

The Bubble is Bursting!

For many who own property or want to own property, it can be hard to believe that what is seen as the safest and most emotionally satisfying investment they could make may turn out to be the greatest scam of the 21st century.

Even today, people in the property business will continue to claim that the property market only ever goes up. They admit there are the occasional downturns, but in general they only see property going up in the end.

THE GREAT PROPERTY PONZI SCAM IS BASED UPON FIAT CURRENCIES, CORRUPT POLITICIANS, BANKSTERS, MORTGAGE BROKERS (SALESMEN), AND GREEDY BUYERS!

The question I have for all of these players is simple. If property only goes up, then why have there been so many resources thrown at the property market to keep it alive?

For instance, all over the world, interest rates are deliberately kept low, politicians campaign for everyone to own a property, banks are forced to lend to people, and social justice groups demand a house for everyone while there are so many homeless.

I will explain this in more detail later in this book, but for now the only premise that advocates of property investment have to support their claim that "property always increases in value" is that there is a massive demand for property and not enough supply; this is what is driving property prices up, to the degree they do rise.

Don't get me wrong—I love property and think it should be part of any balanced investment strategy. What I don't think is right is the way the entire property market operates as a giant Ponzi scam. I don't like what will happen to the average person who will be hurt by the fall in property prices that is coming, and that there will be those who will swoop in like vultures and gobble up these properties for little to nothing. The former owners will then become the new renters.

Don't let your dream become your worst nightmare

The truth is that all over the world, property prices are falling—from the U.S. to China. Prices in Australia and Canada will be next. Property prices in Australia and China will be hardest hit, and ironically these two countries are very strong trading partners.

China relies on a supply of materials from Australia to feed the so-called manufacturing boom in China; Australia relies on Chinese money for its economy. Heaven forbid the day the world stops and China no longer produces goods. What would happen to the Australian economy—and Australian property?

Are you afraid to contemplate such a real event happening? The fact is, it is happening right now before our very eyes.

The U.S. is broke; therefore China will produce less, and that means Australia will get less money. (This global free trade is a real killer when things go south.)

If you don't wake up soon, your property will be worth much less than you think it is. That will turn your dream into your worst nightmare.

House Prices Worldwide

Let's look at what some home price valuations are around the world, and look at the price to income ratio.

Home Price Valuations

Country	Price to Income
Hong Kong	14.1
China (Hong Kong)	11.4
Australia	7.1
New Zealand	6.4
United Kingdom	5.1
Canada	4.6
Ireland	4.8
United States	3.3

Source: 2011 Demographia International Housing Affordability Survey

My first thoughts about the above data is that no one statistic will complete a full picture of any investment asset. However, it is very interesting to look at the chart above, as it refers to the price of a property compared to the income earned by the buyers. This is sometimes referred to as affordability of property.

Housing Affordability Worldwide

Let's look at one of the main drivers of property being housing affordability, and see what that tells us. Just look at the U.S. in the chart above. Though Americans are definitely still experiencing falling home prices, the price to income ratios are 3.3. Let's examine what that means.

Before I start talking about income, let me define median household income. According to the U.S. Census Bureau, "median household income" is defined as "the amount which divides the income distribution into two equal groups, half having income above that amount, and half having income below that amount."

So if the median household income in America is U.S. $48,000, then according to the chart above, the average American is buying a house for around 3.3 times that, or U.S. $158,400.

Let's take the table above and add in some average salary estimates for each country.

Home Price Valuations

Country	Price to Income	Wage	Median Price
Australia	7.1	$68,435	$485,888
Hong Kong	14.1	$32,100	$452,610
United Kingdom	5.1	$58,000	$295,000
New Zealand	6.4	$40,712	$260,556
Ireland	4.8	$47,985	$230,328
Canada	4.6	$42,000	$193,200
United States	3.3	$48,000	$158,400
China	11.4	$10,000	$111,000

Source: 2011 Demographia International Housing Affordability Survey – amended by me!

Australia has a median house price of around $485,888 based upon a 7.1 ratio, yet in the past the price-to-income ratio was around 3, and banks themselves only like lending 33 percent of a person's income to service a loan.

For a moment, let me use 1970's price-to-income ratio of 3, and apply it to today's median income of $68,435. What would the average house price in Australia be at that price-to-income ratio? It would be (wait for it…drum roll please…) $205,305! Yet today's average house price in Australia is actually $485,888, reflecting the massive property bubble that will burst soon.

When this bubble bursts, the average house price in Australia will reduce over the next five years to the $205,305 I spoke of above. That's a reduction of $280,583 on today's prices, or a massive 58 percent drop in value.

As a side note, the most affordable city in the U.S. is Atlanta. With a price-to-income ratio of 2.3, in Atlanta a $48,000 average wage means a house costs $110,400. Have you seen some of these homes? They are really nice.

Okay, don't throw the book away yet. In Chapter 5 you'll learn more about why I chose the 1970s rather than any other period in time. The 1970s is when things really began to change.

Bear with me and keep reading, as your questions will be answered, and the answers will surprise you.

Chapter 3

THE FINE LINE OF

SUCCESS

A Little Story of People Being Gullible

Let me tell you a story that may sound familiar to you. A mate rang me one day and asked what I was doing on Friday. He had just had a fantastic telephone call from a guy who was making 10 percent per month return on investment (ROI), guaranteed.

Given that I was always open to making money, I was inquisitive as to how someone could make 120 percent per year. That's a really good ROI.

So off I went to see my friend and this guy from ABC Pty Ltd, who was to explain to me how the rich people were making money. This person could never meet us at his office, because of course he never had one.

He also turned up in an old run-down Holden, yet he was supposed to show me how to make money!

Then out came the laptop, and let the math lessons begin. "Wow, what great software," I thought, having built my own mortgage brokers' software. I asked basic programming questions, but the guy never had a clue what I was talking about.

The graphs and projections were amazing. Then the stories and testimonials made this almost believable. The sales pitch continued, and after an hour or so I was dumb enough to sign up for a $2,000 course.

I justified spending the money as part of my education, and given what I know today the investment was actually well worth it. Had I been even more naïve, I would have actually started trading and lost thousands more.

In hindsight, I should have asked the hard questions, like: where did the fund operate out of? How could they make so much money and not pay taxes? (In other words, was it offshore?)

The game was and always will be a Ponzi scheme, with new people's money coming in to pay the previous investors' returns on their investments. Even a friend of mine who ran a managed fund with over $1 billion under management said it was hard enough for the professionals to make a return on their money, let alone make 10 percent per month.

From people I have spoken to over the years, I have learned that there are schemes that simply fail, and then there are schemes that are downright Ponzi scams. The truly greedy people run with these, and although promised a new world of riches and wealth, they just end up losing their money.

A bit of financial education would help!

Educating yourself is a never-ending process for most people. It is *what* you get educated in that makes you wealthy or not. Many people can tell you all the sports statistics for a particular sport, or who was the best singer on American Idol. Might it be better to learn and pay attention to some financial basics?

Others get educated in University as doctors, lawyers and engineers. Don't get me wrong, I have nothing against a good education if you just want a job. The bottom line is that such people are book-wise and not street-wise, so most of them play the game according to the rules today.

Educating oneself can mean the difference between success and failure. I should know, as I have made many mistakes, only to learn from them and reapply my experience for success. If you can learn from someone like me who has made lots of mistakes, then your path to success will be a lot faster. In fact, if I was back in my twenties now and had this book, I would be able to save myself a lot of money and mistakes, and would have become successful even sooner.

Don't listen to the media, your mates or your advisors
Most people in your life want good things for you, but many are also afraid that you may get ahead of them because you know something they do not.

Most people in the world are what I call "sheeple" who do little or no challenging of the system. They may jump up and down on occasion for a good cause, but most just go along with the big Ponzi scam that most people operate under. This is why 95 percent of people will end up poor.

Over a lifetime of work, most people are "takers"—that is, they rely on the government for help in retirement. This is pretty scary when you consider that the average pension is less than U.S.

$20,000 per year. Just go down the street and meet an old lady or gentleman who is on a pension, and ask him/her how life is today. I very much doubt that he or she feels well taken care of or secure, or has much to live for besides perhaps grandchildren.

Why do so many people stay poor? It's pretty simple: they toe the line, they follow the rules made by the rich, and they don't think they can make a difference. In essence, people stay poor because they don't know how to get rich.

Back in 1970, most people felt wealthy because they owned their homes, and this is exactly what the politicians wanted them to feel. But the reality is much different today as the cracks in the property market begin to show.

So what do poor people do? Most focus energy on going to school, getting a job, then buying a home, having some kids and then retiring in comfort.

Can you relate to this? Is this what you have done all your life? I know I have. But now I am truly awakened to this scam to which we are all subjected. The only difference between you and me may be a real financial education.

Chapter 4
THE HISTORY OF MONEY

At this point, you need a history lesson on money.

Most people don't know much about the history of money or the way it is created. So what is money?

Money is anything that is generally accepted as payment for goods, services, and repayment of debts. The main uses of money are as a medium of exchange, a unit of account, and a store of value. The dominant form of money is currency.

All *modern* money is debt, created when a central or private bank makes a loan. So the amount of money in society is equal to the amount of debt (total debt, not just government debt).

Barter

From man's existence, one of the first forms of exchange was the barter system, whereby people traded one product for another. So if a baker needed food he would barter a trade of his bread for the farmer's food.

This created the concept of intrinsic value, which is the key to understanding the various forms of money that evolved from the barter process.

A faster, more efficient means of exchange was needed, so money evolved into commodities. This form of trade, despite its limitations, was good for avoiding the taxman.

Commodity Money

Commodity money is represented by items such as food that have intrinsic value and hence have been used as a medium of exchange.

Man then learned how to refine precious metals such as iron, copper, tin, and bronze. Merchants freely traded these new metals. Values were originally decided by how much the metal weighed.

These metals were useful because they were not perishable and not too hard to carry.

Gold and silver over the years have been the most prevalent of the metals accepted as money.

Receipted Money

Next, the goldsmiths experimented with paper money. For most people it was too hard to carry around gold coins, so goldsmiths encouraged people to leave their gold with them in exchange for a written receipt, which entitled the owner to withdraw the gold at any time.

Later, goldsmiths add the words "PAY THE BEARER ON DEMAND" to the receipt, so that the owner of the gold could actually sell it to another person, who then presented the receipt to the goldsmith and picked up the gold.

Fractional Money

The goldsmiths soon realised that few depositors actually came in to collect their gold. This gave them the idea to lend out the gold they held on behalf of depositors, in order to make more profit.

In the early days, most goldsmiths were Christians and thus could not lend money and charge interest. This practice was called *usuary* and was not allowed by the Church.

The Jews had a similar restriction, but also had a loophole. While a Jew could not charge interest on a loan to another Jew, they could charge interest on a loan to a Christian.

This is how the first goldsmiths started lending out the gold to potential borrowers.

Then the depositors found out what the goldsmiths were doing, so they demanded part of the action in order for the Goldsmiths to legally do what they were doing.

Hence goldsmiths began to act as loan brokers on behalf of their depositors. Over time this unsocial practice was legistimised by the governments of the day, and the goldsmiths evolved into banks.

Fiat Money

This is paper money decreed by law as legal tender, not backed by any gold or silver. Basically the government makes a law that this paper must be accepted as legal tender for goods and services.

჻

Chapter 5

YOU HAVE BEEN PLAYED

All the President's Men

Every country worldwide has a similar timeline, ending in a similar result, that involves promoting property to give the illusion of wealth to people. Let's look at what happened in America as a guide to how you have been played into investing into this Great Property Ponzi Scheme.

1913—The Federal Reserve is born

In 1910, some of the most powerful and richest men in America journeyed off to Jekyll Island off the coast of Georgia. These men were bankers, not politicians, and they drafted up the blueprint of America's third attempt at a central bank to enslave Americans.

In 1913, President Woodrow Wilson did the unthinkable. He allowed this third attempt to form a central bank in America—now known as the Federal Reserve—to succeed.

These *Banksters*, as I like to call them, created the Federal Reserve system that is the backbone of today's failed monetary system, which regulates and controls your hard-earned money. "The Fed" determines the price you pay for a house or a car, even how much you can earn.

The Federal Reserve was to be a cartel of bankers privately selected by the wealthiest elite of the time. Their aim was simple.

Control the monetary system; hence control the banks, and enslave the people to debt.

One hundred years on, and people are feeling the effects of the Federal Reserve. There is nothing federal about the Federal Reserve. It is a private corporation—not federal—nor has it any reserves for the people.

The Federal Reserve is unaccountable to the American public, yet it regulates the price you pay for property and shares. It does this by controlling the supply of money via the printing presses, and the price of money through interest rates.

In the past 100 years, the American dollar has lost over 90 percent of its value thanks to the Federal Reserve.

1971—America and the world get off the gold standard

In 1971, President Richard Nixon changed the rules of money by taking U.S. dollar off the gold standard. He did this without the approval of Congress. Prior to this, the U.S. government could only print money that was equal to its gold reserves.

America was going bankrupt, so Nixon took away the gold standard and started the printing presses to print U.S. dollars. Thanks to this, inflation took off, and so did the artificial value of assets, including housing and shares.

The middle class became millionaires as house prices increased. The banks started throwing even more money at them via credit cards, car loans, and home loans. Money became cheap and easy.

This started the concept of using your home equity as an ATM for paying off debts and encouraging more spending—all based upon one basic premise, that "house prices always go up in value."

The removal of the gold standard now means that the world is on fiat currency, where central banks can print money as they wish backed by nothing but their "guarantee."

1974—Retirement Planning

In 1974, under President Gerald Ford, the U.S. Congress passed the Employee Retirement Income Security Act (ERISA), which led to retirement vehicles like the 401(k) (or superannuation, as it is known in England and Australia).

This effectively forces employees to put their retirement funds in the stock market, therefore transferring control of your retirement money to the Banksters on Wall Street.

This caused the number of financial advisors to explode, as someone was needed to help steer your money into shares and property to perpetuate the Ponzi schemes that the share market and property market truly are.

In fact, many teachers, nurses and even truck drivers became financial advisors. So one minute you're a truck driver and the next you are looking after my money?

I don't think so.

No wonder people lose money. I say: trust no one and look after your own money. To be fair, there are a few good trusted advisors out there, but good luck finding them; if you do, treat them like gold.

(Also, if you are looking at working with a financial advisor, get them to show you how they make *their* money!)

1999—The Glass Steagall Act is repealed

In 1999 President Bill Clinton is his wisdom decided to repeal the Glass Steagall Act, to allow commercial banks to buy up investment banks. This started the rush to use your money for risky investments.

The Glass Steagall Act was passed during the Great Depression in 1933. This Act prevented commercial banks from buying investment banks, to protect your money from speculative investment by the greedy Banksters.

The repeal of the Glass Steagall Act took away this protection, allowing banks to leverage your money in unsafe ways at outrageous ratios that I will explain shortly. They took the risk away from banks and put it on you. Local banks no longer are restricted to make sure they invest safely and wisely.

It is interesting to be aware of who supported President Clinton in this decision: people like Robert Rubin and Larry Summers (President Obama consultants) and Timothy Geithner, current U.S. Treasury secretary under President Obama.

The same Banksters triggered the financial crisis so as to combine savings and investment banks together. This accelerated the sale of financial derivatives that will continue to make the Banksters money while causing you and me to suffer.

"Derivatives are like weapons of mass destruction."
- Warren Buffet

Derivatives are financial instruments whose value is linked to something else. They enable investors and institutions to bet on virtually anything, from interest rates or exchange rates to commodities. They are used to speculate, hedge, or leverage. They are a multi-trillion dollar market and are totally unregulated, thanks to a 2000 amendment by Senator Phil Gramm that was slipped last-minute into an appropriations bill, prohibiting federal agencies from regulating the financial derivatives industry.

2004—Banks set free

On April 24, 2004, U.S. Treasury Secretary Henry Paulson, a former Goldman Sachs boss, argued to the U.S. Securities and Exchange Commission that all borrowing restraints on banks should be abolished.

The banks were freed up to use the money you gave them for safekeeping to go crazy in the derivatives market with massive bets.

Today all this cheap easy credit has resulted in over U.S. $1.4 quad trillion (that's a trillion trillion!) worth of derivatives.

How the hell is anyone going to settle these bets? There is just no way this will continue, and it will crash hard.

2007—Subprime borrowers; U.S. housing crisis is born

In 2007, a new type of borrower was named: "subprime borrower," a person who borrowed money for a house that he could not afford. Some of these borrowers had no job, no income, and no assets (known as the NINJA loans); other were part of the middle class that wanted to speculate and make a quick buck.

These people were borrowing huge amounts of money with no thought to risk. This set up America for the housing crisis in late 2008.

Duped since 1970

So all through the years since 1970, politicians have done their best to drive your money and easy credit from the banks into the property market, so as to keep the prices going up and keep everyone happy.

The end result of this is over U.S. $14 trillion in national debt, over 26 million people unemployed, and property prices that have plummeted and continue to fall to this day.

It is crucial to understand the importance of this history, as it is what has fuelled the property boom since 1970. Cheap easy credit created out of thin air by the Banksters has been loaned to the government at interest, so that it can spend the money on programs that will not work.

So when you start congratulating yourself on how smart you are for investing in property, take a step back, drop the arrogance and think about one thing.

What if property does not go up all the time? What if it has been artificially supported since 1970, to the point where it will crash harder than ever before and may never recover to the heights you have known?

"Unless we embrace fundamental reforms, we will be caught in a financial storm that will humble this great country as no foreign enemy ever could."
- Ron Paul, U.S. Senator, 2008

Chapter 6

THE DRIVERS OF PROPERTY

What drives property prices?

People have been brainwashed for their entire lives into thinking property prices only go up. They are told that the following factors determine consumer sentiment, which drives people to buy houses:

- Interest Rates
- Demand
- Supply
- Population Growth
- Housing Shortages

The property promoters don't like discussing real issues, like what has happened to money over time, derivatives, central banks, or fractional reserve lending practices—concepts you may not even have heard of until you read this book.

But despite the property promoters chanting "location, location" as a reason to buy property at high prices, have you ever noticed that the supposedly "best-located" properties are the hardest hit when the downturns happen?

The world has seen a property crash in the U.S., United Kingdom, Spain, Ireland and numerous other countries, and the fall in prices has not stopped there.

Other more optimistic countries like Australia, Canada and China think that they will be immune from property crashes, but this is far from the truth given the underlying worldwide structural issues.

How Property Prices Have Been Manipulated

Property prices worldwide have been rising since the 1970s due to easy cheap money from the Banksters, but along the way, programs such as the below have helped them further:

- Loose credit standards by the Banksters
- Low interest rates
- Limited release of land by governments
- Favorable tax incentives
- High population growth
- Foreign investment rule changes
- Unregulated property promoters and their investment seminars
- Speculative demand fuelled by the perception that prices only go up

These factors have all contributed to the Great Property Ponzi Scam.

Easy Credit

There is only one real driver of property, that being CREDIT both in the supply and pricing. Credit is the most single most powerful driver of property prices.

Fractional Reserve Banking

Let's take a pause and look at this fractional reserve lending really closely. Pay attention, as this is the most important part.

Basically the goldsmiths became wizards and created money out of thin air. This is the fundamental ingredient for the **current monetary system** under which the world's financial markets operate today.

So how is it that money can be created out of thin air, and how does that affect you?

The process by which banks create money is so simple that it is disturbing to the average person who works so hard for his money.

Most people believe that money is created by the government printing presses. This is partially true. The government mint produces the notes and coins we use.

Private corporations known as banks create the vast majority of money via their loans. Each and every time a bank makes a loan, new bank credit is created.

You probably think that the bank lends out money deposited by other people that it actually has in its vaults. But this is not correct. Remember the goldsmiths? The bank actually lends money based upon the borrower's promise to pay it back, like an I.O.U.

The borrower signs the mortgage documents, whereby he promises to pay back the original principal loan and also the interest and fees applicable as per the agreement. If he doesn't pay, he loses the security that was put up for the loan.

So basically the bank creates money out of thin air. Is this too farfetched for you to comprehend? But it's true. The bankers and the government agree to what is known as "the Fractional Reserve System" whereby the bankers agree to be regulated and to only create new money based upon a *percentage* of *actual* deposits held by the bank. (In other words, the reserve needs only to be a *fraction* of actual deposits.) The U.S. requires that banks maintain 10 percent as a statutory reserve, but in some countries the reserve is nil!

Do you know what statutory reserve deposit *your* banks are required to have? Might be worth asking the question, as the lower the reserve, the more likely problems are in the future.

So over the years, *the basic character of money has changed from* **representing a store of value to representing debt**. The government has allowed what is known as fiat (money by decree) currency, which is paper money, to be legalised as acceptance of any debt.

New money is now created when someone takes out a loan. What is worse is that the deposits you make to the bank are actually *you lending money to the bank*—which then turns around and lends out your money *tenfold* based upon the agreed fractional reserve ratio of that bank!

Here in a nutshell is how it works

When the government spends more money than it raises in taxes, it borrows the difference by selling interest-bearing I.O.U.s such as U.S. bonds. Fractional reserve banking allows governments to issue bonds or I.O.U.s to raise cash to cover the shortfall of tax revenue and government spending.

When a U.S. bank buys a U.S. $100 bond, it gets to loan out nearly 10 times that amount, as agreed upon by the government of the day. So not only does the bank get back that $100 investment, plus interest from the federal government, it gets to loan out ten times that amount (that it does not actually have) and charge additional interest on that loan.

That is creating money out of thin air. The bank is making interest on the loan of money it does not have!

The banks are not making just, say, five percent on the $100 investment in U.S. bonds; they are actually making five percent on the $1,000 they have created as new loans, which equates to over 1000 percent interest!

Money is created by Banksters and then loaned back to governments, companies and people like you and me. The loans are backed by the borrower's promise to pay.

No Debt, No Money
Now you know that banks do not lend money but rather create it out of thin air from debt on the borrower's promise to pay. This is really important when you think about it: **No Debt = No Money**.

The monetary system provides debt to people like you and me via banks' creation of money out of thin air, under the authority of the government.

Money breaks us or makes us. Money is the lifeblood of our institutions and our society. Finance affects every part of our lives. Therefore, understanding the monetary system is critical to understand why our lives are the way they are. Not having a financial education may have a serious impact on your ability to become wealthy.

The media make it so intimidating to challenge the status quo that most people go along with the propaganda.

The monetary system runs so deep it starts at school, attacking us when we leave school and when we get our first job. Then it continues to enslave us until the day we stop work and look forward to retirement—only to find out that our so-called retirement money has been destroyed.

School fails to teach us how to make money, how to manage money, or how to invest money. School does not teach us how to make money with money . It does not even teach the basics.

That is the bad news. The good news is that it is not hard to actually teach yourself how to make money, how to manage money—and best of all, how to make even more money with money you make.

Your Money Is Not Safe In The Bank
I have already explained what money is, and that what you think is money is really debt.

Think about this for a moment: when you have money, you keep it in your bank account, right? Then you use it for buying stuff along the way, and keep the rest sitting there in the bank account.

Did you know that your money in that bank is actually an "UNSECURED LOAN" to the bank and if the bank went bust, you wouldn't get the money back?

The government keeps us in the dark so we don't all run down to the bank and take our money out at the first news of any problems. This is called a "run on the bank."

Yes, this happens. In the 1929 Depression, President Roosevelt had to call a bank holiday to stop the so-called run on the banks. Or look at Northern Rock Bank in England on 14th September 2007, when people were lining up to get their money out.

Banks and Fractional Reserve Lending

Remember how the banks take your deposit money and lend it 10 or 100 times into the system? Their doing so means the money *we* hold is actually debt. This is trouble.

Most people borrow money for big items like cars, shares, or houses. And this is where the problems begin.

As time goes on, the cycle is repeated. The initial deposit is loaned out at 10 times its value. Then the recipent buys something like, I don't know, say...a HOUSE! Then he sees the value of the house go up, so he uses it like an ATM, borrowing against equity. Bingo: more money is "created" and used to buy, say, a car. The car seller puts that money into *his* bank, and off we go again.

To truly understand this concept, take the time to visit a Canadian fellow called Paul Grignon at his website **http://www. moneyasdebt.net/**

Just tell Paul Grignon I sent you.

༺ঃ

Chapter 7

THE FEDERAL RESERVE

Creation of the Monster

America has had three attempts to create a U.S. Central Bank, with the first being in 1781 when the "Bank of North America" was created.

The second attempt was in 1791 called "The First Bank of the United States."

Both banks were privately owned and riddled with fraud. By increasing inflation, both these banks fell out of favor and soon ceased operations.

In desperation, J.P Morgan—arguably the most influential banker in the early 1900s—caused a crisis by claiming a bank was in trouble. The consequent run on this bank in 1907 caused a panic in the financial markets.

A congressional commission headed up by Senator Nelson Aldrich (who had ties to the Morgan banking cartel and even ended up marrying into the Rockefeller family), came up with the recommendation that America needed a central bank to stop a repeat of the 1907 panic.

This was the foot in the door that the central bankers needed. Senator Aldrich successfully promoted the cause and America's third attempt at a central bank—The Federal Reserve—was successful.

This third attempt to establish a central bank in America came in November 1910, when international bankers secretly met for nine days at a vacation estate belonging to J.P Morgan on Jekyll Island, off the coast of Georgia in the U.S.

Their main purpose was to form an international banking cartel aimed at the creation of a central bank in America (like the Bank of England, which was the central bank in Great Britain).

It was at this meeting that the draft of what is now the "Federal Reserve Act" was completed. *This document was written by bankers, not lawyers.*

The banking houses attending were J.P Morgan, Rockefeller, Rothschild and Warburg.

The Banksters had four main objectives:
1. Reduce bank competition
2. Make easy credit available to everyone
3. Get bailed out by governments if any problems
4. Convince people that their objectives were in the people's interest

Look at the bailouts of Wall Street today and see if you think the objectives have been achieved. Wall Street banks lost nearly U.S. $100 billion in 2008, and received U.S. $175 billion in government bailouts.

These same banks paid out U.S. $35 billion in bonuses and kept the remaining U.S. $40 billion as pure profit. One in five bailout dollars was pure subsidy from the government to the banks.

In 1913, President Woodrow Wilson came to power with the backing of the banking cartel, on the basis that he had pre-agreed to sign in the new Federal Reserve Act. It was two days before Christmas in 1913 that the Act was passed.

Just look at what even President Woodrow Wilson said after he had allowed the creation of this new central bank in America.

"Our great industrial nation is controlled by a system of credit. Our system of credit is privately concentrated. The growth of the nation therefore and all our activities are in the hands of a few men...who necessarily, by very reason of their own limitations, chill and check and destroy genuine economic freedom.

"We have come to be one of the worst-ruled, one of the most completely controlled and dominated governments in the civilized world. No government by free opinion, no longer a government by conviction and the vote of the majority, but a government by the opinion and the duress of small groups of dominant men."

- Woodrow Wilson (Former U.S. President)

Who owns the Federal Reserve?

Despite the name, the Federal Reserve is *not* federally owned, nor does it hold any government reserves.

The Federal Reserve System virtually controls the nation's monetary system, yet it is accountable to no one.

It has no budget, it is subject to no audit, and no Congressional Committee knows of or can truly supervise its operations.

It has no legal responsibility to be transparent or accountable to the U.S. government or the people of the United States of America.

It is private shareholders who influence the Federal Reserve—not the U.S. government.

So who owns the Federal Reserve?

12 Regional Federal Reserve banks essentially own the Federal Reserve. They are in:

- Boston
- New York
- Philadelphia
- Cleveland
- Richmond
- Atlanta
- Chicago
- St Louis
- Minneapolis
- Kansas City
- Dallas
- San Francisco

And who are the main corporations behind the 12 Federal Reserve Regional Banks?

- Citigroup Inc.
- J.P Morgan Chase
- Bank of America Corporation

- Wachovia Corporation
- Wells Fargo & Company
- Bank One Corporation
- Taunus Corporation
- Fleet Boston Financial
- U.S. Bancorp
- ABN Amro North American Holding Company
- HSBC North America Inc.
- SunTrust Banks, Inc.
- National City Corporation
- Fifth Third Bancorp
- BB&T Corporation

And who are the main individuals behind these banks?

- The Rothschilds of England and Germany
- Moses Seif of Italy
- Lazard Freres of France
- The Warburgs of Germany
- Kuhn-Loeb of Germany
- Goldman-Sachs of the United States
- Lehman Brothers of the United States (now defunct)
- Rockefellers of the United States

"It is well that the people of the nation do not understand our banking and monetary system, for if they did, I believe there would be a revolution before tomorrow morning."
- Henry Ford (Former U.S.President)

The Fed prints money that belongs to Americans and then loans it back to them and charge interest for the pleasure.

Sorry, my bad, the Fed does not print money!

Throughout this book I refer to the U.S. Federal Reserve printing money. They did at one time do just that.

Now, however, as U.S. Fed Chairman Ben Bernanke explained on the TV program "60 Minutes," the U.S. Federal Reserve does not print money.

He is right and he is wrong. You see, thanks to technology today, the U.S. Federal Reserve does not have to print the actual dollar notes—now they can just "credit the bank accounts."

In essence, U.S. printing presses have been swapped for a keyboard on a computer—but the end result is still the same.

How the Federal Reserve manages your money

The Federal Reserve systems allows for the creation of loans into the banking system. Most of the loans are for companies or people, and backed by security like a house or car.

This creation of money and the money supply allows control over an economy. To reduce the amount of money in the economy, the process would simply be reversed.

The Fed sells bonds to the public and the money flows back to the purchaser's local bank.

So a sale of $1 million in bonds to the public by the Fed brings back $10 million from the economy. That's fractional reserve lending.

One of the main weapons wielded by the Fed is the *discount rate* (also referred to as the *discount window*) which is the interest rate charged to commercial banks on the loans they receive from their regional Federal Reserve Banks.

To expand credit, the Fed lowers the discount rate; or to contract, it raises the discount rate.

The Federal Reserve Bank *causes* the BOOMS and BUSTS!

The public was told that the Fed would *stabilise* the economic boom and busts, but history has proven the complete opposite.

From 1914-1919, the money supply doubled. Then in 1920, the Fed called in loans, causing a massive financial panic and triggering runs on banks; some 5400 banks outside of the Fed reserve system collapsed, thus further consolidating the Fed's monopoly on banking.

But 1920 was just a warm-up. From 1921-1929, the Fed again increased the money supply by over 60 percent, and once again made extensive loans to banks and businesses. This period also brought the creation of margin loans, whereby a person could put 10 percent down and borrow the rest to buy shares; this became very popular in the roaring twenties.

The catch with this loan was that it could be called in at any time—an event called a *margin call*—which meant the person had to sell the shares for whatever price he could get to meet the debt.

Before October 1929, insiders exited the stock market knowing what was about to happen. On October 24, 1929, the bankers who had issued the margin loans started calling them in, sparking a massive sell-off of shares and the collapse of over 16,000 banks.

This could be termed the greatest robbery of all time. What is worst was that the Fed went one step further, and this time rather than printing more money and stimulating the economy, it actually *contracted* the economy, causing the 1929 Depression.

There is so much evidence that these Federal Reserve policies led to the crash of 1929. The practices of expansion and contraction by the Federal Reserve contributed to events that were designed to trigger the 1929 Great Depression, and continue that pain in the future.

The expansion of the money supply as a means of helping the economy of England pay for World War I, and the resulting wave of speculation in stocks allowed by margin loans and real estate, shows enough evidence that the Federal Reserve had foreknowledge of the crash.

While so many lost so much in this crash, there is always someone at the other end who makes money out of the losses.

In this case, these were the friends of the Federal Reserve, who were forewarned as to what was coming.

In any future depression, there will again be those who will lose fortunes and those who will make fortunes. Which one will you be?

"Some of the biggest men in the United States, in the field of commerce and manufacture, are afraid of something. They know there is a power somewhere, so organised, so subtle, so watchful, so interlocked, so complete, so persuasive that they had better not speak above their breath when the speak above their breath in condemnation of it."

- Thomas Woodrow Wilson (Former President of the United States)

The Federal Reserve and the Fall of the U.S. Dollar

The Federal Reserve creates inflation when it issues U.S. dollars backed by government debt. Since 1913, when Congress created the Federal Reserve, America has lost 96 percent of its purchasing power due to inflation.

From 1913 to 2001, the national debt grew to U.S. $6 trillion in 88 years. Over the next three years, it climbed to U.S. $7 trillion dollars in 2004. In just one year it climbed sharply **to** over U.S. $11 trillion dollars. In 2011, the U.S. National Debt has now exceeded U.S. $14 trillion.

The acceleration of the national debt is alarming. The corresponding loss of your purchasing power may also accelerate in the near future.

The Federal Reserve is a Giant Ponzi Scheme

The Federal Reserve, the quasi-autonomous body that controls the U.S. money supply, is a "Ponzi scheme" that created bubble after bubble in the U.S. economy and needs to be held accountable for its actions. It is spending the future taxes of U.S. citizens (some not even born as yet!) This is one great Ponzi scheme that even Bernie Madoff would be proud of.

The Federal Reserve and its shenanigans should horrify every single American, because what it is currently doing is little but downright criminal activity that will cost most Americans dearly.

Remember all Ponzi schemes fall under their own weight just like Bernie Madoff's did, and so too this Federal Reserve Ponzi scam will fall hard, with the end casualties being you and me worldwide.

Monetising the Debt

In August 2009, the U.S. government starting monetising debt—that is, it started buying back its own bonds within 10 days of their actual sale. The U.S. Federal Reserve bought back over 47 percent of the seven-year bonds it had sold to investors like China, Saudi Arabia, and Japan, at the same time that Timothy Geithner (U.S. Secretary of the Treasury) asked Congress to raise the debt ceiling.

On March 6, 2009, Federal Reserve chairman Ben Bernanke declared that the Fed would not monetise any U.S. debt, yet by September 16, 2009, some U.S. $5 billion of U.S. debt had been monetised.

The Fed is printing money to buy U.S. bonds as a means of faking the U.S. Treasury's ability to raise outside capital from places like China or other international buyers. It used to be overseas investors would buy bonds (our debt). In reality, today the U.S. credit card is well and truly cut off.

Effectively the U.S. Federal Reserve is printing money to buy U.S. treasury bonds that cannot be sold to international investors, due to investors seeing America as an economic risk (and rightly so).

What is wrong with this, you may ask? Zimbabwe did this, and in 2008 they experienced hyperinflation. Secondly, only the government can repay the debt, and it must repay it in one of two ways: **higher taxes** or **inflation.**

In Gold We Trust

In 1957, the U.S. added the words "in God we Trust" to the U.S. dollar. By 1971, after President Nixon took the U.S. off the gold standard, the purchasing power of money had diminished as the printing presses kept on printing money.

The true value of most fiat currencies, like the U.S. dollar and that of most countries today, will reduce to zero over time.

Just look at how much gold you could buy with U.S. dollars over the years. In 1970 you could have bought an ounce of gold for around **U.S. $35,** by 2009 the same ounce of gold cost around **U.S. $900,** and by 2011 the price of ounce of gold has reached over **U.S. $1400.**

This just shows the loss of value of the U.S. dollar as the country tries to print its way out of economic woes.

෩෧

Chapter 8

WHO CAN YOU TRUST?

"Trust me, I am a financial advisor!"

In 2008, the world awakened to the Global Financial Crisis that shook the world. Established investment banks like Lehman Brothers went broke.

In fact, my wife and I were on a flight one day and she saw the financials for Lehman Brothers in a magazine. She turned to me and said "Wow, look at this; this business looks so strong."

We smiled at each other as we dreamed of owning such a wealthy company. Only later did we see how misleading those figures really were, when we saw the media reports that Lehman Brothers was now broke.

Also in 2008, Merrill Lynch, the largest stock brokerage in America, went bankrupt and was sold to Bank of America. These are the trusted financial advisors looking after American's life savings, and they went bankrupt?

Then look at other financial advisors that had to get bailed out. When financial advisors go bust, it's scary. These guys have our money and they are supposed to not only be financial gurus but also the utmost trusted people in finance.

Not only did they go broke, suggesting incompetence, but surely along the way they knew they were in trouble—so where was the trust in telling us what was happening?

Perhaps they *cannot* really be trusted, as their main interest is themselves, not you. I was at one time a mortgage broker in Australia and had arguably the fastest growing mortgage brokerage business in Australia. I did not like what I saw.

Mortgage brokers in fact have an inherent interest in making money from their dealings with you, and no real care as to what would happen to you if you could not pay the mortgage. That is the only explanation as to why it was ever possible to get a loan for 100 percent of the value of a property.

As for financial advisors, I still cannot understand how anyone can pay them commissions to look after their retirement savings, and then watch their hard-earned money lose value every day.

There is no relationship between *your* risk and *their* income. This is why they are happy to keep switching your investments or just advise you to buy, buy, buy.

A Ponzi Scheme
Another thing that annoys me about the so-called experts is that they want you to send them your money, which they will invest on your behalf, rather than show you how they have made *their* money.

Like property and the Federal Reserve, this too is a Ponzi scheme.

I keep talking about Ponzi schemes. What *is* a Ponzi scheme? A Ponzi scheme is a term named after Charles Ponzi (1882-1949) who was considered one of the greatest swindlers of all time.

A Ponzi scheme is an investment fraud in which the early investors are paid by money from new investors, who are lured in via the promise of high returns. Bernie Madoff's infamous swindle was an example of a Ponzi scheme.

Today the property market is a Ponzi scheme in which new buyers prop up the earlier buyers' property prices. What happens if new buyers stop buying? I can tell you what happens: the price of your property goes down.

We saw this in the mortgage market in the U.S. in 2007. Old investors and new ones panicked and wanted their money back, and the whole world went spiraling downwards.

To "save the world," the Federal Reserve started printing money to keep the Ponzi scam going.

This whole scam only works as long as the average person acts like a zombie and doesn't become financially educated.

The Smartest People in the World

Let's go back to the 2008 Global Financial Crisis and see who actually predicted this would happen, and what did they do to help you survive.

The number of people who saw the GFC coming were actually few and far between. The number of people (including "experts") who did *not* see it coming are too numerous.

I was one who actually saw the GFC coming and sold my mortgage brokerage business in 2005 before the proverbial hit the fan.

I am just an average bloke who saw the signs. Just as now I see the same situation headed toward us with the property market, which is why now I don't own property.

Chapter 9

DO YOU STILL WANT TO BUY PROPERTY?

How to invest in property despite my warnings

Suppose you have read this book up until this page and you *still* want to invest in property. All right, then, go on and buy the property—but do it the smart way at least.

After reading this book, you should be selling any property you have, or at least paying off any debt you have so as to maximise your chance of keeping the property.

Remember, the Banksters are not nice people. So if you fall behind in your repayments, or they just decide to revalue your property in a falling market, it is always best to have more equity than debt. Otherwise, you will give the bank the reason it needs to foreclose on your home and sell you up!

Yes, those nice guys at the bank who loaned you the money in the first place, the ones who begged you to take out the loan—they are the same ones who want to sell you up and take the property.

To avoid any foreclosure, you must be able to make your repayments on time and ensure that the property is worth more than the debt.

Start doing your own math and work out what your property would be worth if it lost 50 percent of its value. Then deduct your mortgage and work out whether you have your head above water.

Another thing on which to work out the math is what would happen to you if interest rates went up to 10 percent or more, like they did in the late 1980s. Could you afford to make your repayments on the loan if interest rates went to those levels?

Have you slit your wrists yet? Don't, because that does no good. But one more thing that may depress you further. What if you lost your job? You know, like the 26 million or more Americans now looking for work (unless they have given up)?

If you lose your job, then you are really up the creek without a paddle. Then those same smiling bankers who loaned you money will come over to your house and tell you everything will be fine. Actually, no—they will be the first to change the locks and throw you and your family out on the street.

The bottom line is make sure your loan is *less than* half the amount of the *real value* of your property. NOT what you think it is worth, but what a professional appraiser would value your property at, just as it is now. Spend the $300 for that appraisal and find out. Then at least you will know where you stand—and if the math does not work in your favor, you can either rent the property out or sell it (your call).

Personally, I have sold all my property, as I know what is coming. I am not willing to risk my money with a bunch of Banksters who are controlling this Ponzi scam.

I am happy to rent for a couple of years—why not? I can rent a beautiful home for two to five years and watch the carnage, with no effect to my property portfolio, and then come back in after the crash and buy up property for half the price.

Sounds good to me.

Buying Property In America

Right now, property prices in America are still going down, and thousands of overseas investors (especially from Australia) are being flown in to buy up what is described as "cheap property with great returns."

Now, I have been to America, and have seen for myself some of these properties. Some do look really liveable, but this type of investment relies on some underlying assumptions with which I am not comfortable.

These basic (but I think faulty) premises are: (1) that the property values will go back up, (2) that renters are happy to pay the rents, and (3) perhaps the worst one, that the renters will keep their jobs.

I have news for people who want to invest in American property in which Americans will not even invest: you are going to lose your money bigtime!

When you buy your U.S. $50,000 house in America, and you get a 20 percent return via the U.S. $200 per week in rent, it all sounds really good—a no-brainer, in fact.

But if you actually flew to the United States and did your research, then you would know that Americans are not buying houses. In fact, in America, homeowners and agents can barely even give them away.

Just ask yourself this question: if these properties are such a good deal, why don't the *Americans* buy them? In fact, given that interest rates in America are so low, the average American should have no problem buying property—especially as the price-to-income ratio is around 3:1, which is low compared to Australia at 7:1.

Something is just not adding up. It may be something the locals know that you, as the investor, don't know.

The sad fact is that in most cases, you could not sell these U.S. $50,000 properties for U.S. $25,000. As for the renters, in some parts of America people are actually abandoning their properties because the neighbourhoods are going to the dogs. Good luck collecting the rent there.

Some reasons why Americans are not buying property:

- There exists a possibility that American property prices could go still lower.
- The cost of health insurance is rising rapidly.
- More employers are ending or reducing coverage of employee health care.
- The number of Americans without health insurance is on the rise.
- Unemployment is on the rise.
- Average annual wage in America is U.S. $26,261.

- In 2011, some 40 percent of all Americans cut back on spending.
- In 2011, some 2.6 million Americans dropped into poverty.
- The U.S. national debt is $14.2 trillion as of this writing.
- Divided by the number of U.S. citizens, that's U.S. $47,634 per citizen.
- Allocated among U.S. taxpayers, this debt is U.S. $132,462 per taxpayer.

While you may not see a deficit of $132,462 on your personal balance sheet or get a bill for the full amount tomorrow, don't feel complacent. In the future, the U.S. government will doubtless find ways to extract money from your pockets to pay "your share" of its astronomical debt, even if you did not personally condone the national spending that caused this debt!

Please check out the scary statistics at <u>www.usdebtclock.org</u>!

No wonder Americans don't want to buy property now—or *can't*—despite being advised that it is a great investment.

Chapter 10
CHANGE YOUR THINKING

Poor people think and act like this:
1. They go to school and learn nothing real about money.
2. They get a job, work hard and save some money.
3. They buy a house, thinking it is their greatest investment.
4. They believe that property and shares always go up.
5. They want to retire and live happily ever after.
6. They think that if things go bad, the government will look after you.

Your property is NOT an asset

One of the main challenges for all of us is recognizing that OUR HOME IS NOT AN ASSET. If you buy a house to live in, it does not create income for you.

With property comes expenses, such as mortgage, maintenance and operating costs such as energy, etc.

If you buy a home to live in, then you are getting a liability and not an asset. Once you understand this, you will start the journey to becoming financially secure.

Investment property is different, as you have the tenant and the taxman help you to pay the bills.

"It is not the asset class that determines if something is an asset. What determines if something is an asset is the direction of the cash flow. If cash flows into your pocket, it is an asset. If cash flows out of your pocket, it's a liability."

- Robert Kiyosaki

Different Investor Types

Now take a minute and decide which type of person and investor you are.

1.   THE ZOMBIE
I am just a zombie with no idea and I don't care

I just go to work if I have a job, and I have a friend who is rich. The government can be trusted, and it will look after me if I get in trouble.

2.   THE SAVER
I am a Saver

I work hard, save some money from time to time, and squirrel it away in my bank. I hope to buy a home or a car one day.

3.   THE KNOW-IT-ALL
I am a professional and know what I am doing

I have a well-paid job, a good home I live in (with a high mortgage), and know what one needs to know about investing.

4.   THE MONEY WARRIOR
I am learning the truth every day

I go to work, use tools to budget, work on generating more cash flow, and continue to challenge the status quo.

Money Warriors think and act like this:

- Investing in themselves and getting a real financial education.
- Working smart and not hard.
- Getting out of BAD debt and using GOOD DEBT for investment.
- Not saving money, but investing in assets that generate positive cash flow.
- Not relying on property or shares going up.
- Not expecting the government to look after them.
- Having enough cash flow to live well in retirement.

"Success is not final, failure is not fatal: it is the courage to continue that counts"
- Winston Churchill

Conclusion

Many people wait for the political or financial systems to change, but this will never happen because the Banksters have too much money and power.

In my opinion, it is easier for me to change my habits than for me to change our leaders or systems.

Congratulations on reading this book. It may well be the first step in your new future. I would personally like to thank you for taking your valuable time to read this book, and hope I have challenged your thinking.

Don't forget to check out **www.moneywarstv.com.**

Good luck with your financial education and pursuit of happiness.

❧

www.ingramcontent.com/pod-product-compliance
Lightning Source LLC
Chambersburg PA
CBHW071252170526
45165CB00003B/1312